EXPANDED EDITION
Grade 2

The *Our Blue Planet* lesson is part of the
Picture-Perfect STEM program K–2 written by the
program authors and includes lessons from their
award-winning series.

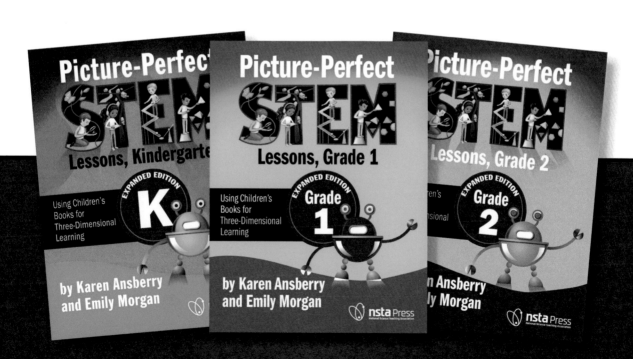

Picture-Perfect **STEM** Lessons, Kindergarten

Using Children's Books for Three-Dimensional Learning

EXPANDED EDITION K

by Karen Ansberry and Emily Morgan

Picture-Perfect **STEM** Lessons, Grade 1

Using Children's Books for Three-Dimensional Learning

EXPANDED EDITION Grade 1

by Karen Ansberry and Emily Morgan

nsta Press
National Science Teaching Association

Picture-Perfect **STEM** Lessons, Grade 2

Using Children's ...nsional

EXPANDED EDITION Grade 2

...n Ansberry ...ly Morgan

nsta Press
National Science Teaching Association

Our Blue Planet

Description

A famous photograph of Earth called "The Blue Marble" introduces the phenomenon that most of our planet is covered in water. By exploring with maps, globes, and satellite images of Earth and reading a book that shares names and descriptions of various bodies of water, students are able to identify both liquid and solid bodies of water (ice) on Earth. Students also use the Google Earth app to take virtual field trips to different places on the planet and to locate the bodies of water closest to their school.

Alignment with the *Next Generation Science Standards*

Performance Expectations
2-ESS2-2: Develop a model to represent the shapes and kinds of land and bodies of water in an area.
2-ESS2-3: Obtain information to identify where water is found on Earth and that it can be solid or liquid.

Science and Engineering Practices	Disciplinary Core Ideas	Crosscutting Concept
Developing and Using Models Develop and/or use a model to represent amounts, relationships, relative scales (bigger, smaller), and/or patterns in the natural and designed world(s). **Obtaining, Evaluating, and Communicating Information** Read grade-appropriate texts and/or use media to obtain scientific and/or technical information to determine patterns in and/or evidence about the natural and designed world(s).	**ESS2.B: Plate Tectonics and Large-Scale System Interactions** Maps show where things are located. One can map the shapes and kinds of land and water in any area. **ESS2.C: The Roles of Water in Earth's Surface Processes** Water is found in the oceans, rivers, lakes, and ponds. Water exists as solid ice and in liquid form. **ETS2.A: Interdependence of Science, Engineering, and Technology** Science and engineering involve the use of tools to observe and measure things.	**Scale, Proportion, and Quantity** Relative scales allow objects to be compared and described (e.g., bigger and smaller; hotter and colder; faster and slower).

Note: The activities in this lesson will help students move toward the performance expectations listed, which is the goal after multiple activities. However, the activities will not by themselves be sufficient to reach the performance expectations.

Featured Picture Books

TITLE: **All the Water in the World**
AUTHOR: **George Ella Lyon**
ILLUSTRATOR: **Katherine Tillotson**
PUBLISHER: **Atheneum Books for Young Readers**
YEAR: **2011**
GENRE: **Narrative Information**
SUMMARY: *Rhythmic language and vibrant artwork describe why "all the water in the world is all the water in the world," which keeps cycling through various forms and places.*

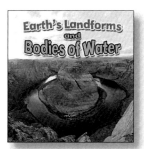

TITLE: **Earth's Landforms and Bodies of Water**
AUTHOR: **Natalie Hyde**
PUBLISHER: **Crabtree**
YEAR: **2015**
GENRE: **Non-Narrative Information**
SUMMARY: *Vivid photography and simple text introduce children to the different landforms and bodies of water that are found on Earth. The book includes ways that maps and globes are used to model Earth's features.*

Time Needed

This lesson will take several class periods. Suggested scheduling is as follows:

Session 1: **Engage** with *All the Water in the World* Read-Aloud and **Explore** with "The Blue Marble" and Google Earth Virtual Field Trip

Session 2: **Explain** with Comparing Bodies of Water and *Earth's Landforms and Bodies of Water* Read-Aloud

Session 3: **Elaborate** with Where's Our Water? and **Evaluate** with Our Blue Planet Place Map

Materials

For "The Blue Marble"

- "The Blue Marble" photograph from *Apollo 17* (see "Websites")
- Globe and world map

For Google Earth Virtual Field Trip

- Google Earth and Google Maps app

For Earth's Landforms and Bodies of Water *Read-Aloud*

- Scissors
- Globe and world map
- Tape or glue

SAFETY
Use caution when handling scissors to avoid puncturing skin.

For Where's Our Water?

- Google Earth and Google Maps apps

For Our Blue Planet Place Map (per student)

- Scissors
- Crayons or markers
- Bodies of Water Cards (uncut)
- Cutout strips of Ocean Cards
- 9 × 12 in. white card stock or construction paper
- Glue

Student Pages

- Google Earth Virtual Field Trip
- Bodies of Water
- Bodies of Water Cards
- Ocean Cards
- Our Blue Planet Place Map
- STEM Everywhere

Background for Teachers

In 1972, NASA took a photograph that changed the way we see our world. In fact, it is one of the most widely distributed photographs of all time. This photo of Earth, taken as the *Apollo 17* astronauts were heading to the Moon, gave us a new perspective on our planet. It reminded the astronauts of a swirly blue glass marble, so the photograph was aptly titled "The Blue Marble."

The blue color of our planet is due to the abundance of water, which gives off blue light upon reflection. Nearly three-fourths (about 71%) of the surface of Earth is covered in water, and most of that water (about 96.5%) is contained within the ocean as *salt water*. The greatest volume of *freshwater* on Earth is not located in rivers or lakes. It is located underground or frozen in *glaciers* and *polar ice caps*. In fact, only about 1% of all the water on Earth is accessible freshwater. Our water is precious—all that's here is all we have. Thus, understanding Earth's water is a key concept in K–12 science education.

An *ocean* is a large, deep body of salt water. There is really just one ocean that covers our planet, but explorers and oceanographers have divided the world ocean into five named regions: Atlantic, Pacific, Indian, Arctic, and Southern. All these ocean regions flow into one another (which is why

THE BLUE MARBLE

OCEAN REGIONS

there is truly only one ocean). There used to be only four named oceans, but since 2000, most countries recognize the Southern Ocean as the fifth ocean. (Note that older classroom maps and globes may not have the Southern Ocean labeled.). Also, many people use the words *ocean* and *sea* to mean the same thing, but geographically, a sea is a large body of salt water that is completely or partly surrounded by land (often part of an ocean).

This lesson also addresses several bodies of freshwater: lakes, ponds, rivers, streams, canals, and glaciers. A *lake* is a large body of (usually) freshwater surrounded on all sides by land, whereas a *pond* is a smaller body of still water. A *river* is a long, narrow body of water that flows into a lake or the ocean. A *stream* is a general term for a small body of moving water. Depending on its location or certain characteristics, a stream may be referred to as a river, branch, brook, creek, or other term. A *canal* is a humanmade waterway that connects two bodies of water. Canals can be either freshwater or salt water depending on the bodies of water they connect. A *glacier* is a dense layer of slow-flowing ice that forms over many years, sometimes centuries. A glacier differs from an iceberg, which is a huge body of ice that floats on water. Understanding how bodies of water are named can be tricky. For example, the Dead Sea is actually a saltwater lake, the Sea of Galilee is actually a freshwater lake, and there are many more exceptions to the naming conventions that people have used throughout history. For students, learning the names of bodies of water is not as important as their understanding that (1) water can be found as a liquid and a solid in a wide variety of bodies, (2) these bodies can be located on maps, and (3) technology can help us map our planet.

Since "The Blue Planet" photo was taken, there have been great advances in photographing and mapping our planet. Satellites orbiting Earth can take pictures, and global positioning systems (GPS) can locate us (or at least our smartphones) on maps. In this lesson, students are engaged in the science and engineering practice (SEP) of developing and using models as they use digital models, such as Google Earth and Google Maps, to locate and compare different bodies of water on Earth. The composite images on Google Earth are made using photographs taken by satellites orbiting our planet,

4

airplanes that fly over Earth, and even Google cars that drive around and take "street view" footage. This technology allows us to explore our planet from the comfort of our classrooms. Finally, students make their own "place-map" model of our blue planet, showing the locations of the five named ocean regions. The SEP of obtaining, evaluating, and communicating information is used as students compare the ideas about bodies of water they put together from their experience with Google Earth to the information in a nonfiction book. The crosscutting concept (CCC) of scale, proportion, and quantity is incorporated as students compare the sizes of different bodies of water on Earth and how that relates to the way the body of water is classified (e.g., ocean, sea, lake, pond).

Using maps to locate different kinds of land and water in grades K–2 sets a foundation on which students can build in grades 3–5. In the upper elementary grades, students not only use maps to locate land and water features on Earth but also begin to explore the patterns of different landforms on Earth that are often formed along the boundaries between oceans and continents.

Learning Progressions

Below are the disciplinary core idea (DCI) grade band endpoints for grades K–2 and 3–5. These are provided to show how student understanding of the DCIs in this lesson will progress in future grade levels.

DCIs	Grades K–2	Grades 3–5
ESS1.C: The History of Planet Earth	• Some events happen very quickly; others occur very slowly, over a time period much longer than one can observe.	• Local, regional, and global patterns of rock formations reveal changes over time due to Earth forces such as earthquakes. The presence and location of certain fossil types indicate the order in which rock layers were formed.
ESS2.A: Earth Materials and Systems	• Wind and water can change the shape of the land..	• Rainfall helps to shape the land and affects the types of living things found in a region. Water, ice, wind, living organisms, and gravity break rocks, soils, and sediments into smaller particles and move them around.
ETS1.C: Optimizing the Design Solution	• Because there is always more than one possible solution to a problem, it is useful to compare and test designs.	• Different solutions need to be tested in order to determine which of them best solves the problem, given the criteria and the constraints.

Source: Willard, T., ed. 2015. *The NSTA quick-reference guide to the* NGSS: *Elementary school.* Arlington, VA: NSTA Press.

engage

All the Water in the World Read-Aloud

*Inferring*

> Connecting to the Common Core
> **Reading: Literature**
> KEY IDEAS AND DETAILS: 2.2

Show students the cover of *All the Water in the World* and introduce the author, George Ella Lyon, and the illustrator, Katherine Tillotson. Read the first line, which says, "All the water in the world is all the water in the world." *Ask*

? What do you think the author means by this? (Answers will vary.)

Continue reading the book aloud and stop after reading page 11, which says, "Water doesn't come. It goes. Around." *Ask*

? What do you think the author means by those lines? (Answers will vary.)

Have students listen for the answers to the two questions you've asked as you continue reading the book to the end. From the reading, they should recognize that all the water in the world has been here before in different places and different forms. There is no other supply of water—all the water in the world is all the water we have. After reading the book, *ask*

? Where is water found on Earth? (Answers will vary.)

Tell students that they will be learning all about all the water in the world!

explore

"The Blue Marble"

*Inferring*

Project the famous NASA photograph titled "The Blue Marble" (see the "Websites" section). *Ask*

? What do you observe about this picture? (Answers will vary.)

? How do you think it was made? (Answers will vary.)

Explain that this photograph of Earth was taken in 1972 by the *Apollo 17* astronauts as they were traveling to the Moon. The photograph is famous because it was the first to show an almost fully illuminated Earth from the view of a spacecraft. This was achieved because the astronauts had the Sun behind them when they captured the image. The photograph also marks the first time the south polar ice cap was photographed from space. An interesting fact is that nobody knows for sure which astronaut actually took the picture! What we do know for sure is that the photograph had a powerful effect on people and changed the way they thought about Earth.

Questioning

Ask

? What are you wondering about the photograph? (Answers will vary.)

? What makes the blue color on Earth? (water)

? What makes the brown and green colors on Earth? (land)

? What makes the white colors on Earth? (clouds and ice)

? Why do you think the photograph was titled "The Blue Marble?" (Earth's shape is similar to a marble, Earth is mostly blue, and the swirls of clouds look like the swirls on some marbles.)

? From looking at this photo, can you tell whether Earth is mostly land or mostly water?

National Science Teaching Association

(Answers will vary, but students should realize that the photo shows only one side of Earth, so it is impossible to tell by looking at it.)

To find out whether Earth is mostly land or mostly water, students will need to see the whole Earth, not just one side. Use a globe to show students a three-dimensional view of Earth. Tell students that a globe is a *model* of Earth. *Ask*

? How is a globe like the real Earth? (It is round, it spins, etc.)

? How is it different? (It is much smaller, it is on a stand, etc.)

Point out that some globes have an arrow somewhere that shows the direction Earth spins on its axis. If you are looking down on the North Pole, a globe should turn counterclockwise to represent how Earth spins in space. Spin the globe slowly in a counterclockwise direction, and *ask*

? How does this model of Earth compare with "The Blue Marble" photograph? (The globe is round, but the photo is flat; the globe is not a real picture, but the photo is a real picture; the globe does not show clouds, but the photo does show clouds; both the globe and the photo show that Earth has a round shape; etc.)

? On the globe, does it look like Earth is mostly land or mostly water? (Answers will vary, but by looking at a globe, it is more evident that Earth is mostly water.)

? Is it possible to travel by water all the way around the globe without crossing any land? (Yes. Have a volunteer demonstrate this by placing one finger on an ocean region and moving it completely around the globe without crossing any landforms.)

Students should notice by observing the globe that the amount of water on Earth greatly exceeds the amount of land. (They will learn from the reading in the explain phase of the lesson that water covers three-quarters of Earth's surface and that most of the water is in Earth's ocean.)

Google Earth Virtual Field Trip

(*Note:* Depending on the availability of technology, this activity could be done as a whole group with the application projected on a screen or in pairs on computers or handheld devices.)

Tell students that they are going on a field trip! This is not a real field trip; it is a "virtual" field trip to explore Earth's water using a computer application called Google Earth. Explain that the images on the Google Earth app are made with *satellite* cameras that orbit Earth, airplanes that fly above Earth, and even cars that drive around to take photographs. Engineers at Google put these photographs together to create this digital model so that we can "fly" around our planet and see what different places actually look like.

> **SEP: Developing and Using Models**
> Develop and/or use a model to represent amounts, relationships, relative scales, and/or patterns in the natural world.

The search feature on Google Earth allows students to enter the name of a place and "fly" there. Point out that sometimes the red placemark icon that shows up is not located exactly on the body

USING GOOGLE EARTH

of water they have entered in the search box, so they will need to zoom out or zoom in (using a two-finger pinch) to get a better view. Students will need to enter the country or city (found in parentheses) for rivers and ponds to more accurately locate those bodies of water.

Give each student a copy of the Google Earth Virtual Field Trip student pages. In pairs, groups, or as a whole class, use the Google Earth app to "fly" to all of the different bodies of water listed on the student pages. There are ocean regions, seas, lakes, rivers, canals, ponds, and glaciers to visit. Have students make observations of each type of body of water and note similarities and differences. Then have pairs of students develop a definition for each body of water based on the evidence they collected from the virtual field trip and write it in the "Our Definition" column. For example, "An ocean is … a large body of water that connects to other bodies of water around Earth."

> **CCC: Scale, Proportion, and Quantity**
> Relative scales allow objects and events to be compared and described. (e.g. warmer, cooler)

explain

Comparing Bodies of Water

After students have had a chance to locate the various bodies of water and develop working definitions for them, ask the following questions:

Ocean Regions and Seas

? Based on the evidence from the virtual field trip, how did you define *ocean*? (Answers will vary.)

? How did you define *sea*? (Answers will vary.)

? Which is larger, an ocean or a sea? (An ocean is larger than a sea.)

? What is your evidence from the virtual field trip? (Answers will vary.)

? Have you been to an ocean or sea? (Answers will vary.) Could you see to the other side? (no) Why not? (It is too far, they are too big, and Earth's surface is curved.)

? How many oceans do you think there are on Earth? (Answers will vary, but in the reading that follows, they will learn that Earth has one ocean with five named regions.)

Lakes, Rivers, Canals, and Ponds

? How did you define *lake*? (Answers will vary.)

? How did you define *river*? (Answers will vary.)

? How is a river different from a lake? (A river is longer and thinner than most lakes. Rivers are connected to other bodies of water.)

? What is your evidence from the virtual field trip? (Answers will vary.)

? How did you define *canal*? (Answers will vary.)

? How is a canal different from a river? (A canal usually has straighter sides and goes in more of a straight line.)

? What is your evidence from the virtual field trip? (Answers will vary.)

? How did you define *pond*? (Answers will vary.)

? How is a pond different from a lake? (It is smaller.)

? What is your evidence from the virtual field trip? (Answers will vary.)

Glaciers

? How did you define *glacier*? (Answers will vary.)

? Why do you think a glacier is considered a body of water? (It is made of frozen water.)

? Does a glacier flow like a river? (Answers will vary, but students may have observed the grooves formed by the flowing ice. In the reading that follows, students will learn that glaciers are thick layers of slowly moving ice.)

Earth's Landforms and Bodies of Water Read-Aloud

Connecting to the Common Core
Language
VOCABULARY ACQUISITION AND USE: 2.4

Next, show students the cover of *Earth's Landforms and Bodies of Water*, and tell them that this book will help them learn more about some of the different bodies of water on Earth. Read pages 4–5 aloud. Point out the map of the world at the top of page 5. *Ask*

? How do you think this map was made? (using photographs taken by satellites)

> **SEP: Obtaining, Evaluating, and Communicating Information**
> Read grade-appropriate texts and/or use media to obtain scientific and/or technical information to determine patterns in and/or evidence about the natural world.

Skip pages 6–13, which are about rocks, soil, and landforms (you may want to revisit these pages later). Then explain that the rest of the book describes several bodies of water, but before you continue reading, you would like the class to try to match these different bodies of water to their descriptions.

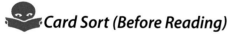 ## Card Sort (Before Reading)

Give each student a copy of the Bodies of Water and the Bodies of Water Cards student pages. Have them cut out the cards and place each one next to the description they think matches. Encourage students to think of how some of these bodies of water looked on the virtual field trip. If they are

not sure, they can guess at this point. Let students know that they will have a chance to move their cards after you read the book aloud.

After students have placed their cards, read aloud page 14 of *Earth's Landforms and Bodies of Water*, which defines an ocean as a large, deep body of salt water and explains that most of the water in the world is located in the five ocean regions on Earth. Stop and look at a large map of the world. Have students locate all five ocean regions. Use a globe to show the same bodies of water, and point out that older globes and maps may not have the Southern Ocean labeled because that region wasn't named until the year 2000. Then have students observe how the Pacific Ocean appears on the globe versus on the map. Explain that it is hard to show on a map that the Pacific Ocean is actually in between Asia and the American continents. Then remind students that, although the names all include *ocean*, there is really only *one* ocean on Earth because all ocean water can flow freely around the globe and mix with other ocean water (which you demonstrated in the explore phase). *Ask*

? If there is really only one "world ocean," why do you think five oceans have been named? (It is convenient to separate the "world ocean" geographically by naming different parts of it; having only one named ocean would make it confusing for sailors, mapmakers, and people in general.)

Continue reading to the end of the book. After reading, *ask*

? Which two bodies of water on the Bodies of Water Cards were not described in the book? (seas and canals)

? Which description do you think goes with *sea*? (description 6)

Explain that sometimes people use the terms *ocean* and *sea* interchangeably, but there is a difference. Seas are smaller than oceans and are usually located where the land and the ocean meet. Seas are partly or totally enclosed by land. The terms

can get tricky, though. Some bodies of water, such as the Dead Sea, are actually salt water lakes! *Ask*

? Which description do you think goes with *canal*? (description 7)

? Can you think of other bodies of water that were not described in the book? (bays, gulfs, straits, wetlands, puddles, etc.)

Card Sort (After Reading)

After reading the book, go through the answers together and have students move their cards, if necessary. When students have all of the cards correctly placed, they can glue or tape them into the appropriate boxes. The answer key is in Table 17.1.

Table 17.1. Answer Key for Bodies of Water

Description	Card
1. A large, deep body of salt water	Ocean
2. A long, narrow body of moving water that flows into a lake or the ocean	River
3. A large body of (usually) freshwater surrounded by land on all sides	Lake
4. A small body of still water	Pond
5. A thick layer of moving ice	Glacier
6. A large body of salt water that is completely or partly surrounded by land; often part of the ocean	Sea
7. An artificial waterway that connects two bodies of water	Canal

Questioning

Then *ask*

? Which bodies of water are salt water? (oceans and seas)

? Which bodies of water are freshwater? (streams, rivers, lakes, ponds, and glaciers)

? There are actually some salt water rivers and lakes on Earth. Do you know of any lakes that are salt water? (Some students may be familiar with Utah's Great Salt Lake or other saline lakes around the world.)

? Are canals made of salt water or freshwater? (It depends on the bodies of water they connect.)

? Do you think most of the water on Earth is salt water or freshwater? (salt water, because most of Earth's water is in the ocean)

? Do we drink freshwater or salt water? (freshwater)

Explain that it is important to conserve and protect our freshwater sources, because although Earth is three-fourths water, only a tiny fraction of it is drinkable! Our water is precious. All that's here is all we have. *Ask*

? What are some ways we can conserve, or save, our water? (Answers will vary but may include turning off the faucet when we brush our teeth, not leaving water running, being careful not to litter or pollute water, using less water on lawns by planting drought-resistant plants, etc.)

elaborate

Where's Our Water?

Students can apply their knowledge of different bodies of water by locating and identifying the nearest bodies of water to their school using the Google Maps app. For this activity, you will be using the map layer instead of the satellite layer. The bodies of water will be easier to see in the map view than in the satellite view. Demonstrate how to locate your school in Google Maps by following these steps:

1. Enter the school's address in the "search" field of Google Maps.

2. Make sure you are viewing the map layer.

3. Explain that, on this map, blue represents water.

> **SEP: Developing and Using Models**
> Develop and/or use a model to represent amounts, relationships, relative scales, and/or patterns in the natural world.

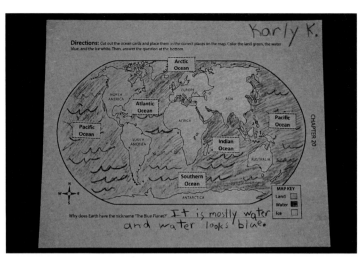

OUR BLUE PLANET PLACE MAP

The following activity could be done as a class or with partners: Slowly zoom out and stop when you see a body of water. Determine what kind of body of water it is by its size, shape, and name. Keep zooming out, pausing to take note of all the bodies of water on the map. Together, see if you can locate which ocean, sea, stream, river, lake, pond, canal, and glacier is closest to the school.

evaluate

Our Blue Planet Place Map

Synthesizing

Give each student a copy of the Our Blue Planet Place Map student page and a strip of Ocean Cards to cut out. Have them refer to a classroom globe, map, or Google Earth to correctly place the names of all five of Earth's ocean regions. (Point out that Pacific Ocean will be used twice, and remind students that some maps and globes may not have the Southern Ocean labeled.) Then have students color the water blue, the land a different color, and the ice white. They can then fill in the map key showing the colors they used for areas of land, water, and ice. Finally, have them answer the question at the bottom, which asks, "Why does Earth have the nickname 'The Blue Planet'?" When students have completed their place maps, they can glue them onto a 9 × 12-inch piece of white card stock or construction paper. If possible, laminate the maps and then send them home with students to act as a daily visual reminder that "all the water in the world is all the water in the world"!

> **SEP: Developing and Using Models**
> Develop and/or use a model to represent amounts, relationships, relative scales, and/or patterns in the natural world.

STEM Everywhere

Give students the STEM Everywhere student page as a way to involve their families and extend their learning. They can do the activity with an adult helper and share their results with the class. If students do not have access to the internet at home, you may choose to have them complete this activity at school.

Opportunities for Differentiated Instruction

This box lists questions and challenges related to the lesson that students may select to research, investigate, or innovate. Students may also use the questions as examples to help them generate their own questions. These questions can help you move your students from the teacher-directed investigation to engaging in the science and engineering practices in a more student-directed format.

Extra Support

For students who are struggling to meet the lesson objectives, provide a question and guide them in the process of collecting research or help them design procedures or solutions.

Extensions

For students with high interest or who have already met the lesson objectives, have them choose a question (or pose their own question), conduct their own research, and design their own procedures or solutions.

After selecting one of the questions in the box or formulating their own question, students can individually or collaboratively make predictions, design investigations or surveys to test their predictions, collect evidence, devise explanations, design solutions, or examine related resources. They can communicate their findings through a science notebook, at a poster session or gallery walk, or by producing a media project.

Research

Have students brainstorm researchable questions:

? How much of Earth's water is frozen?

? What was the first satellite in space? How many humanmade satellites are now orbiting Earth?

? What is the longest river in the world? Largest lake? Largest ocean?

Investigate

Have students brainstorm testable questions to be solved through science or math:

? Which is longer, the Nile River or the Amazon River? What is the difference in length?

? Locate the nearest ocean on a map. Find a city or town on the coast that might be fun to visit. Type your home address into Google Maps or another map program, and use the "Directions" feature. Type in the name of your coastal destination. How many miles away is it? How long would it take to get there by car? How much longer would it take to get there if you walked?

? Survey your friends and family: Would you rather live on the shore of a river, a lake, or an ocean? What would be the benefits and risks of your choice? Graph the results, then analyze your graph. What can you conclude?

Continued

Opportunities for Differentiated Instruction (continued)

Innovate

Have students brainstorm problems to be solved through engineering:

? Can you use Google Earth to plan your dream vacation?

? Can you design a model to show the shapes and kinds of land and bodies of water in your state or country?

? Can you design a way to keep a beach from eroding into the ocean?

Websites

 "The Blue Marble" From *Apollo 17* (1972)
   https://earthobservatory.nasa.gov/ images/2181/the-blue-marble

 Google Earth
   www.google.com/earth

 Google Maps
   www.google.com/maps

More Books to Read

Dorros, A. 1991. *Follow the water from brook to ocean.* New York: HarperCollins.
   Summary: This Let's-Read-and-Find-Out Science book explains how water flows from brooks, to streams, to rivers, over waterfalls, and through canyons and dams to eventually reach the ocean.

Lindstrom, C. 2020. *We are water protectors.* New York: Roaring Book Press.
   Summary: Inspired by the many Indigenous-led movements across North America, poetic text and stunning illustrations express the importance of protecting and preserving Earth's water.

Olien, R. 2016. *Water sources.* Mankato, MN: Capstone Press.
   Summary: This fact-filled book will introduce young readers to rivers, oceans, lakes, groundwater, and other bodies of water. Water on Earth in the form of ice is also covered.

Paul, M. 2015. *Water is water: A book about the water cycle.* New York: Roaring Brook Press.
   Summary: Simple, poetic text and dreamy illustrations follow a group of children as they experience the different phases of the water cycle.

Name: _____

Google Earth Virtual Field Trip

Directions: Use the Google Earth search feature to "fly" to the following bodies of water on Earth. Zoom in or zoom out with a two-finger pinch to get a good look! Put a check (✓) in the box after you have seen each one. Next, write a definition for each body of water that is based on your observations.

Body of Water	Our Definition
1. **Ocean Regions** ☐ Atlantic Ocean ☐ Pacific Ocean ☐ Arctic Ocean ☐ Indian Ocean ☐ Southern Ocean	**An *ocean* is …**
2. **Seas** ☐ Caribbean Sea ☐ Mediterranean Sea	**A *sea* is …**
3. **Lakes** ☐ Lake Superior ☐ Lake Victoria	**A *lake* is …**

National Science Teaching Association

Body of Water	Our Definition
4. **Rivers** ☐ Nile River (Cairo) ☐ Yangtze River (Wuhan)	**A *river* is …**
5. **Canals** ☐ Panama Canal ☐ Suez Canal	**A *canal* is …**
6. **Ponds** ☐ Walden Pond (Massachusetts) ☐ Antonelli Pond (California)	**A *pond* is …**
7. **Glaciers** ☐ Pine Island Glacier ☐ Bering Glacier	**A *glacier* is …**

Bodies of Water

Directions: Cut out the Bodies of Water Cards and match them to the correct description.

Description	Picture
1. A large, deep body of salt water	
2. A long, narrow body of moving water that flows into a lake or the ocean	
3. A large body of (usually) freshwater surrounded by land on all sides	

Description	Picture
4. A small body of still water	
5. A thick layer of moving ice	
6. A large body of salt water that is completely or partly surrounded by land; often part of the ocean	
7. An artificial waterway that connects two bodies of water	

Bodies of Water Cards

Sea

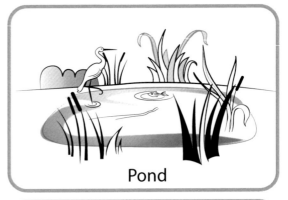

Pond

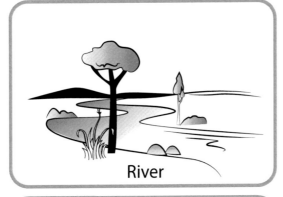

River

Lake

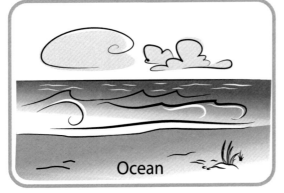

Ocean

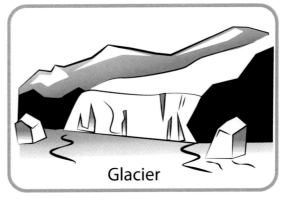

Glacier

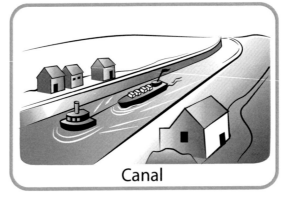

Canal

Ocean Cards

Arctic Ocean	Atlantic Ocean	Indian Ocean	Pacific Ocean	Pacific Ocean	Southern Ocean
Arctic Ocean	Atlantic Ocean	Indian Ocean	Pacific Ocean	Pacific Ocean	Southern Ocean
Arctic Ocean	Atlantic Ocean	Indian Ocean	Pacific Ocean	Pacific Ocean	Southern Ocean
Arctic Ocean	Atlantic Ocean	Indian Ocean	Pacific Ocean	Pacific Ocean	Southern Ocean
Arctic Ocean	Atlantic Ocean	Indian Ocean	Pacific Ocean	Pacific Ocean	Southern Ocean
Arctic Ocean	Atlantic Ocean	Indian Ocean	Pacific Ocean	Pacific Ocean	Southern Ocean
Arctic Ocean	Atlantic Ocean	Indian Ocean	Pacific Ocean	Pacific Ocean	Southern Ocean
Arctic Ocean	Atlantic Ocean	Indian Ocean	Pacific Ocean	Pacific Ocean	Southern Ocean

Our Blue Planet Place Map

Name: _____

Directions: Cut out the Ocean Cards and glue them in the correct places on the map. Color the water blue, the land a different color, and the ice white. Then answer the question at the bottom of the page.

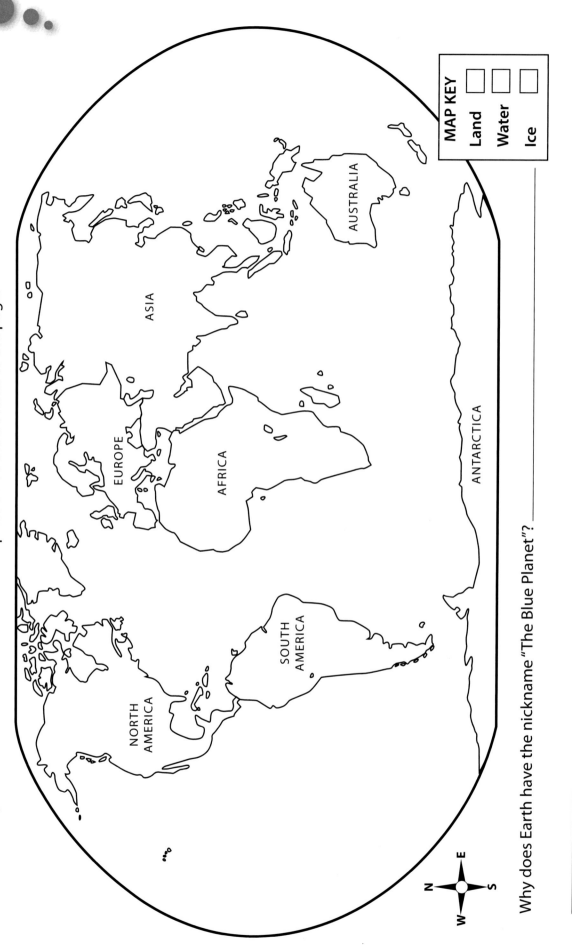

MAP KEY

☐ Land

☐ Water

☐ Ice

ASIA

AUSTRALIA

EUROPE

AFRICA

ANTARCTICA

NORTH AMERICA

SOUTH AMERICA

Why does Earth have the nickname "The Blue Planet"? _____

N E S W

20

STEM Everywhere

Dear Families,

At school, we have been learning about how maps can be used to locate bodies of water on Earth. We used Google Earth to find different oceans, seas, lakes, ponds, and rivers on Earth. We used Google Maps to find the closest body of water to our school. To find out more, ask your learner questions such as:

- What did you learn?
- What was your favorite part of the lesson?
- What are you still wondering?

At home, you can read about how Google Street View technology works. First, read the passage below with an adult helper. Then begin exploring together by following the directions.

About Google Street View

Do you like to look at maps? One kind of map is the Google Street View map, which allows you to view places as if you were standing right there! The photographs you see on these maps are often taken by cameras mounted to the tops of special Google Maps camera cars. But cars can't go everywhere, so sometimes the photos are taken by cameras mounted on bikes, backpacks, boats, or even snowmobiles! The photos are then joined together to make the full 360° pictures you see.

Using this technology, you can relax in the comfort of your own home while you take a virtual walk through your neighborhood. Street View even offers views of national parks and other famous places. Let's take a look!

Continued

Name: _____

Using Google Street View

1. Go to *www.google.com/maps*.

2. Type your address into the box at the top that says, "Search Google Maps," and hit "enter."

3. Does a picture of your home appear below the search box? If so, click on the picture.

4. The picture will expand to full view. Click and drag the picture to explore the 360° view, if possible. What do you observe?

5. Click the back arrow to bring back the search bar. Then try typing a famous place into the search bar, such as Niagara Falls, Old Faithful, the Grand Canyon, or anywhere else you would like to visit! Click on the picture, then click on some of the pictures that may appear below the search bar.

6. Draw a picture of something you observed in the box below.

National Science Teaching Association